*Children learn to read by **reading**, but they need help to begin with.*

When you have read the story on the left-hand pages aloud to the child, go back to the beginning of the book and look at the pictures together.

Encourage children to read the sentences under the pictures. If they don't know a word, give them a chance to 'guess' what it is from the illustrations, before telling them.

There are more suggestions for helping children to learn to read in the *Parent/Teacher* booklet.

British Library Cataloguing in Publication Data
McCullagh, Sheila K.
    The fox and the magician. —(Puddle Lane series).
    I. Title   II. Rowe, Gavin   III. Series
    428.6   PR6063.A165/
    ISBN 0-7214-1072-3

First edition

Published by Ladybird Books Ltd Loughborough Leicestershire UK
Ladybird Books Inc Lewiston Maine 04240 USA

Printed in England

The fox and the Magician

written by SHEILA McCULLAGH
illustrated by GAVIN ROWE

This book belongs to:

Ashley Crayton

Ladybird Books

The Wideawake Mice were all
in the big hole under the hollow tree,
when Chestnut came down the mousehole
from the garden.

"It's time we went out to look for food,"
he said.

"I don't think I can go out this evening,"
said Aunt Matilda.

"Nor can I," said Uncle Maximus.
Uncle Maximus didn't want to go
because he was feeling frightened,
but Aunt Matilda really wasn't very well.

The Wideawake Mice were
in the big hole under the tree.

Aunt Matilda had nearly been eaten
by a fox the evening before.
She had escaped, but
she was still feeling very shaken.
She was very upset, too, because
her dress was all torn and muddy.
All the other mice were growing
more like wood mice every day.
But Aunt Matilda couldn't forget
that she was a Wideawake Mouse.
She liked to look pretty and neat,
and when she looked at her torn dress,
she felt very unhappy.

Aunt Matilda was very upset.

The sun was beginning to set.
There were long shadows in the garden,
as the Wideawake Mice
came out of the hole,
and scattered to look for food.
Chestnut went off to find
the hole down to a crocus bulb
that he had dug the day before.
Aunt Jane went with
Grandfather and Grandmother Mouse,
to look for nuts on the steps
of the Magician's house.
And Jeremy and Miranda went off
to a bush of berries, near the wall.

The Wideawake Mice
went to look for food.

They found the bush without any trouble,
and climbed up, to eat the berries.
They had each eaten three, and
were beginning to think
that a few nuts would be very pleasant,
when Miranda suddenly said,
"Look, Jeremy! What's that?"

Miranda said,
"Look, Jeremy!"

They looked down, and saw a little doll
lying in the long grass below them.
Miranda and Jeremy didn't know it,
but the doll belonged to Gita.
Gita and Sarah had been playing
in the garden that afternoon, and
Gita had dropped the doll
as they were going back to the gate.

Jeremy and Miranda
looked down.
They saw a little doll.

Jeremy and Miranda ran down to the ground
to take a closer look.

"It's like the dolls we used to see
in Mr Wideawake's toy shop," said Jeremy.

"It isn't alive, like us, is it?" asked Miranda.

"Of course it isn't," said Jeremy.
"We only came alive when the Magician
spilt magic dust all over us."

"It's got a lovely dress," said Miranda.
"Let's take it back to Aunt Matilda.
It's just the right size.
A new dress would make her happy again."

"All right," said Jeremy.
They began to pull the doll home,
towards the hollow tree.

"Let's take the doll back
to Aunt Matilda," said Miranda.

15

They had not gone far
when they came to some thick bushes.
The two little mice stopped.
"We shall spoil the dress
if we pull the doll through those,"
said Miranda. "Let's take the dress off,
and leave the doll here."

The two little mice stopped.
"Let's take the dress off,"
said Miranda.

The long grass near the bushes stirred.
Jeremy and Miranda were so excited,
and so busy with the doll,
that they forgot to look and listen.
The grass parted a little.
A long nose sniffed the air, and
two bright eyes looked out.
It was the fox.

It was the fox.

Very quietly, the fox moved
an inch or two forward.
Jeremy and Miranda
still didn't see the fox, and
the fox didn't make a sound.
He stood there, watching.
He stiffened, ready to pounce.

Jeremy and Miranda
didn't see the fox.

There was a sudden flash,
and a noise like a thunderclap.
A ball of fire burst over their heads.
The two little mice leapt to one side,
and hid under a big stone.
The fox jumped back.

The fox jumped back.

The Magician was standing by the bushes.
He looked straight at the fox.
"I hear that you have been hunting
in my garden," he said.
"I have made a rule, and
you must obey it.
You can hunt in the woods, or
in the fields, but **not** in my garden.
If you hurt any animals
who live in my garden,
I shall turn you to stone."

The fox looked up
and saw the Magician.

The fox looked at the Magician
for a few moments.
Then, without a word, he turned
and ran off.
He went back through the hole
he had dug under the garden wall,
and across the fields to the wood.

The fox ran off.
He ran out of the garden
and back to the wood.

"Has he gone?" asked a whiffly-griffly voice.

The Griffle's head appeared over a bush.

"Yes, he's gone," said the Magician.
"And he won't come back to the garden.
But keep a watch for me, Griffle.
I don't want anyone
to hurt the Wideawake Mice.
Look after them for me."

"I don't **like** mice," said the Griffle.
"But the Wideawake Mice are a bit different.
I keep seeing them about in the garden,
and I don't think I mind them
as much as I did at first."

"The Wideawake Mice won't hurt you,"
said the Magician.
He went back to the house,
and the Griffle began
to vanish.

"Look after
the Wideawake Mice,"
said the Magician.

Jeremy peeped out from under the stone.
His whiskers twitched.

"There's no one here," he whispered.
He crept out, and Miranda followed him.

"Are you quite sure the fox has gone?"
asked Miranda, looking all around.

"Didn't you hear what the Magician said?"
asked Jeremy. "We're safe now."

"We must still be very careful,"
said Miranda.
"Who was the Magician talking to?"

"I don't know," said Jeremy.
"But whoever it was, he's gone."

Jeremy looked out.
"There is no one here,"
he said.

"Let's go home," said Miranda.
She picked up the dress, and
Jeremy picked up the doll's hat.
They set off for the hollow tree.

"Let's go home,"
said Miranda.

The other mice were all safely back
in the big hole under the tree.
They had heard the bang, and had
seen the flash, and they had run home
as fast as they could.
Grandfather Mouse and Aunt Jane
were just setting out to look for
Jeremy and Miranda,
when the two little mice
came down the mousehole.

Jeremy and Miranda
came down the mousehole.

When Aunt Matilda heard
what the Magician had said to the fox,
she was so thankful that
she began to feel better at once.
And when she saw the dress and hat
that Jeremy and Miranda had brought back
for her, she was so delighted that
she almost danced over the tree roots.
She put on the dress at once, and
by the time she had had some supper,
she was her old self again.

Aunt Matilda put on the dress.

Before the sun had quite gone down,
Gita and Sarah came back to the garden.
They were looking for Gita's doll.
It was Sarah who found it.

"Look, Gita," she cried, picking it up.
"Here it is. But someone has taken
the doll's dress!
Who could have done that?"

"I don't know, but I think
I can guess," said Gita.
"I once saw a mouse on the garden wall.
She was dressed in a skirt.
The mice who live in this garden
aren't like other mice.
I think they must have taken it."

"Look, Gita," said Sarah.
"Here is the doll."

"I think the mice
must have taken
the dress," said Gita.

"How can we get it back,
if the mice have taken it?" asked Sarah.

"We can't," said Gita. "But
I don't mind a bit.
I can make another dress for the doll.
Let's see if we can see the mice."

But although they looked carefully,
they didn't see any mice that evening.
The Wideawake Mice were all at home,
admiring Aunt Matilda's new dress.

Sarah and Gita
looked for the mice.

Notes for the parent/teacher

When you have read the story, go back to the beginning. Look at each picture and talk about it, pointing to the caption below, and reading it aloud yourself.

Run your finger along under the words as you read, so that the child learns that reading goes from left to right. (You needn't say this in so many words. Children learn many useful things about reading by just reading with you, and it is often better to let them learn by experience, rather than by explanation.) When you next go through the book, encourage the child to read the words and sentences under the illustrations.

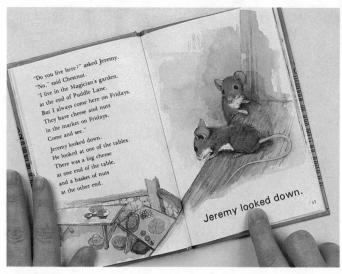

"Do you live here?" asked Jeremy.
"No," said Chestnut.
"I live in the Magician's garden,
at the end of Puddle Lane.
But I always come here on Fridays.
They have cheese and nuts
in the market on Fridays.
Come and see."

Jeremy looked down.
He looked at one of the tables.
There was a big cheese
at one end of the table,
and a basket of nuts
at the other end.

Jeremy looked down.

42

Don't rush in with the word before he* has time to think, but don't leave him struggling for too long. Always encourage him to feel that he is reading successfully, praising him when he does well, and avoiding criticism.

Now turn back to the beginning, and print the child's name in the space on the title page, using ordinary, not capital letters. Let him watch you print it: this is another useful experience.

Children enjoy hearing the same story many times. Read this one as often as the child likes hearing it. The more opportunities he has of looking at the illustrations and **reading** the captions with you, the more he will come to recognise the words. Don't worry if he **remembers** rather than **reads** the captions. This is a normal stage in learning.

If you have a number of books, let him choose which story he would like to have again.

Footnote: In order to avoid the continual "he or she", "him or her", the child is referred to in this book as "he". However, the stories are equally appropriate to boys and girls.

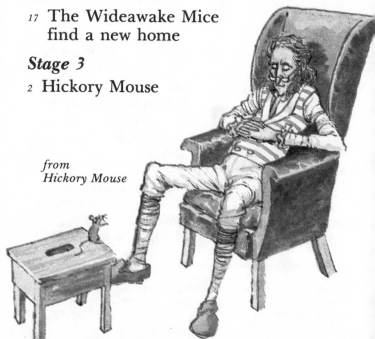

Have you read the stories about how the Wideawake Mice came alive and how they came to live in the mousehole under the hollow tree?

from Hickory Mouse